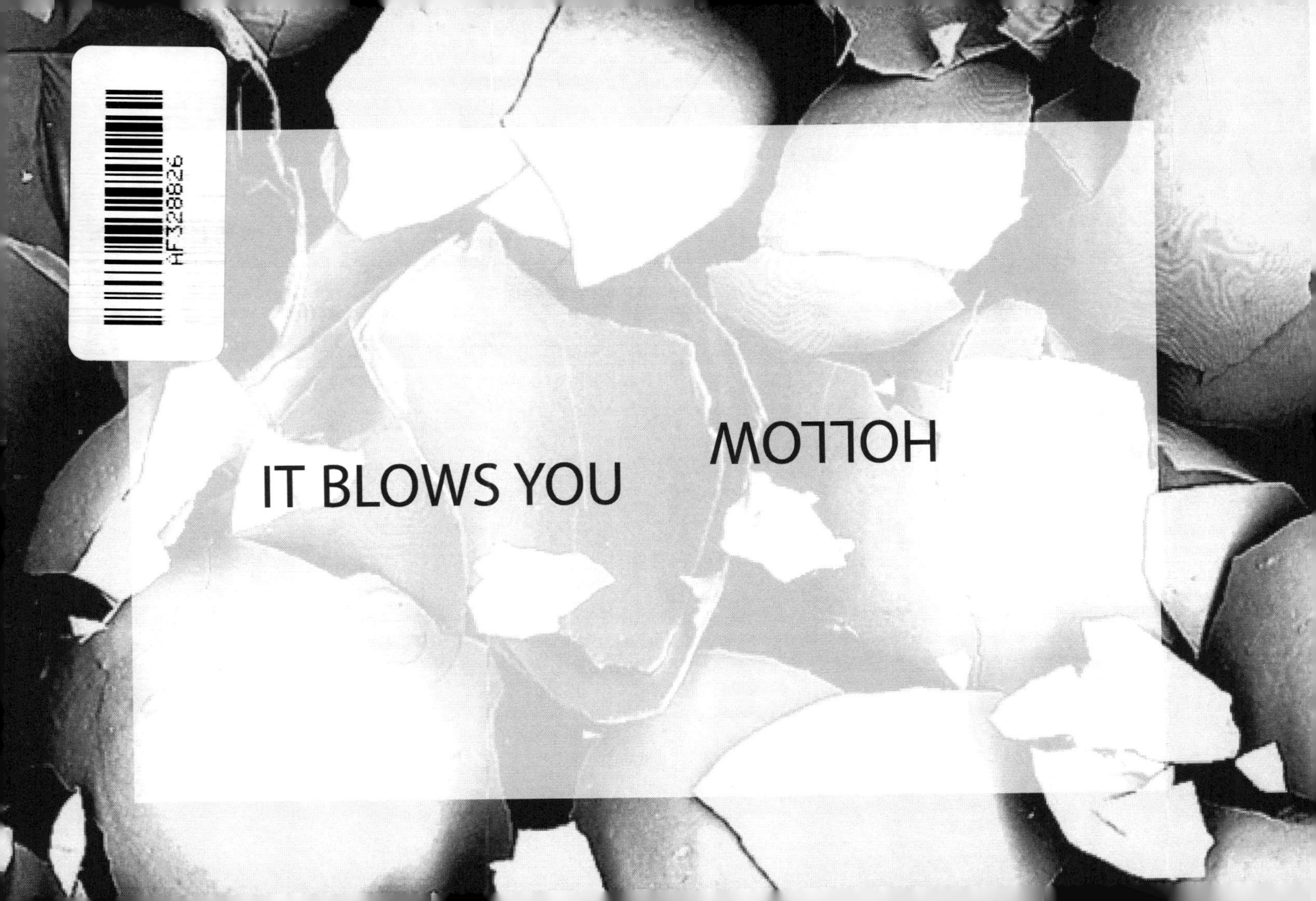
IT BLOWS YOU
HOLLOW
AF328826

The New Issues Press Poetry Series

Editor	Herbert Scott
Associate Editor	David Dodd Lee
Advisory Editors	Nancy Eimers, Mark Halliday William Olsen, J. Allyn Rosser
Assistant to the Editor	Rebecca Beech
Assistant Editors	Scott Bade, Allegra Blake, Becky Cooper, Jeff Greer, Gabrielle Halko, Matthew Hollrah, Nancy Hall James, Alexander Long, Tony Spicer, Bonnie Wozniak
Editorial Assistants	Kevin Oberlin, Matthew Plavnick Diana Valdez
Business Manager	Michele McLaughlin
Fiscal Officer	Marilyn Rowe

The New Issues Press Poetry Series is sponsored by The College
of Arts and Sciences, Western Michigan University, Kalamazoo, Michigan

An Inland Seas Poetry Book

 Inland Seas poetry books are supported by a grant from
The Michigan Council for Arts and Cultural Affairs.

First Edition, 1998.

ISBN: 0-932826-65-2

Library of Congress Cataloging-in-Publication Data:
Seuss, Diane
It Blows You Hollow / Diane Seuss
Library of Congress Catalog Card Number (98-066492)

Art Direction	Tricia Hennessy
Design:	Young Won
Figure Photography:	Alfonso Quiroga
	Untitled, photograph, 10" x 10", gelatin silver print
Production:	Paul Sizer
	The Design Center, Department of Art
	College of Fine Arts
	Western Michigan University
Printing:	Bookcrafters, Chelsea, Michigan

IT BLOWS YOU HOLLOW

DIANE SEUSS

New Issues Press

WESTERN MICHIGAN UNIVERSITY

To Peter and Dylan
In memory of Robert Seuss and Mikel Lindzy

Contents

III

Acknowledgments

Poems in this book have previously appeared in:

Alaska Quarterly Review: "Crucifixions"

Indiana Review: "Hit"

Passages North: "An Inordinate Fondness for Beetles," "What My Son's Haircut Taught Me About Flying," and "Hope"

Poetry Northwest: "Eclipse at Easter," "Landscape"

PrePress Awards Vol. 2: Michigan Voices: "Rising"

Primavera: "What Is There"

Third Coast: "Personality," "It Blows You Hollow"

The epigraph on page 9 is from an article in The Atlantic, January 1992, Vol.269, No.1

I

This Year

Sand Point was under water.
The birch tree that grew on the edge
of the rocks, taken. Deer, I'm told, walked
through town, fur stretched
over trembling bones, trading fear for food.
On the mound of lichen-covered rocks
I call my island, the mouse skull hidden
in a small cave between rocks
is missing this year, after so many years.
The winters are hard up here.

When God comes lumbering out of the woods,
nose to the air, he looks sleek. He pays us
no mind. He's eaten heartily this winter, the black
coat well-oiled. He heads straight
for the roadside to set his claws into the red
nipples of the thimbleberries.

Rising

What do you do after the crucifixion?
The dead body is yellowing within its cave.
What do you do with your time after the pretty one is gone?
Watch the blue heron pick lice out of its wings?
Visit the memory, like a dark red bed hemmed-in by lilacs,
a sexy, lonely place, wrapping your legs around destitute air?

Wander all you want; babble to yourself like a nun
who entered the convent to hide from grief.
Go to an apple orchard and search for the ghost
who doesn't want to be found. Around you the world
is in tremulous flower, wet, wanting to anoint the soft face
and hands of God. You can lie in the high grasses, remembering
the warm skin under your hands, the blue cotton shirt,
the pearly buttons, the clean white winding
sheet, the look in the eyes that said I am dislodging
myself from you, molecule by molecule . . .
Even now you see it all around you:
the heron opening its wings, the mist on the lake,
everything vibrating, evaporating, sparking, dissipating, rising.

An Inordinate Fondness For Beetles

> Asked what years of research had taught him
> about God, the biologist J.B.S. Haldane replied
> that the Creator had an 'inordinate fondness for beetles.'

The beetles have come again.
The shiny black beads have broken and scattered.
The night has shed its scales.
Eat, eat! Feast on the viney world.
Even when we set out the traps and burn
a few hundred of you, we're just
a part of your story.
When you mate on the Virginia Creeper,
when the females crawl out into the grass
and lay the heavy egg sacs down
we know the eggs will survive winter
just as we survived childhood
by our stillness and our silence.
When the beetles march away they will leave
the chewed-out heads of the peace roses.
When they march away, they will leave
my father's bones.
I have a fondness for them, these things that last:
Eaters, grievers, beetles, bones.

The Past Is Golden

When I visit the graveyard
he always comes, this golden
dog, wet from his nights
in the marshlands, smelling
to high heaven of skunk.
His tongue hangs out, dripping
foam. He's hungry; his ribs
ripple the surface of his sides.
He wants me. Not me, but anyone.
He rubs his skunky dampness
against my clothes, leaving
the smell of shame. He will not go away
no matter what I throw at him: stones,
flags, crabapples, small crucifixes
inlaid with bright yellow roses.

Lifelong grief is not enough for this dog.
He wants my devotion, my bed, to eat
off my plate. He wants marriage, he wants me
on a leash. Breath, an open oven in my face,
a smile full of teeth like cloves of garlic.
He wants to cover me in fur, in stink, in foam,
in the slime of bullfrogs and snakes.
He humps my leg, his friendliness a mask
I've seen before: gravediggers, war veterans,
fucking away their rage at the innocent.
His coat's full of things that vex my skin
through my clothes: milkweed seeds,
pine needles, fingernails, bones of swallow,
bones of crow, remnants of summer,
golden fragments of the crown of thorns.

The Casket Company Is On Fire

Meanwhile, the caskets are exploding
musically, one after another.
The children clap out a rhythm;
the teenagers dance close, kissing long
and slow. Can we let it burn?
We've never been this close.
One long ebony box makes a sound
like a voice. When the heat intensifies
the lid opens. We've seen this before,
black iris in the garden, opening
to the sun. Something like loss
is let loose into the world. Shaped
like a person. Hair on fire.
Recognizable face. One of us,
or could be. One who will not have to
lie there, wearing uncomfortable clothes.
The wet weeping.
The hoses are in hand.
The water, like a guard dog
frothing at the mouth, ready
to spring. The choice is the one
we make every morning
but it's never been this clear.
Now the office telephone rings
and rings. Who is it? Some innocent,
putting in an order.

What Is There

What is there to remember?
Spilled milk, milky-skinned dad,
Hazy mom in a yellow blouse
And a crib full of decals—a container.
Later the kid stubs her toe, runs
Away. The feelings were flat
As flatware, weren't they? Or was
She dark and deep, curly-haired
And lonely? Was the loneliness
A cake? Deep brown and damp
With chocolate? Did she cry
With regret, sucking her fingers
Until the cows came home? Was
Her small body tender as a tree-toad's,
Quiet-chested and birdbath-still?
Or was she like the wasps that
Beat the screen door senseless
All summer, hard-assed
And full of poison?

Crucifixions

There are many crucifixions.
Some are quiet, graceful, filigreed.
I watched my father die for six
years—false hope, morphine,

desperate experimentations
with a blue extract
from the periwinkle plant.
I was seven years old,

watching him from the dark
hallway as he looked at himself
in the bathroom mirror, his
fading looks, ears poking

out from the skull, painting
his tongue where he'd accidentally
bit it; and later, when he was
on the telephone, I watched him use

his free hand to catch the spinal fluid
that dripped out of the unhealing incision
on his back with a paper napkin
covered in swans.

Eclipse At Easter

The moon, she is losing
herself. Before, she floated on her back
in the black water, only her round
belly with its blue veins exposed.
Now the shadows have taken her under.
The minnows with their bright blind eyes
explore her body with their mouths.
The ends of her hair sway.
Red Mars is the clasp, holding the strands together.

We walk through wet grasses
with our baskets of eggs, slipping
them into familiar hiding places—
the cleft of the firebush, beneath
the cluster of sage, under dead
leaves, where the snowdrops are beginning
to breathe again. The green buds
of the lilacs claw open our blouses.
Pierced by spruce needles, we bleed.

The children are inside and asleep. Their bodies
are changing beneath the murky sheets,
hair darkening from blonde to brown
to black. Next year they may refuse
to search for what we hide from them.
We'll be alone out here, the drowned
moon's bones knocking against
each other in the current, caught
in the watercress, in the reeds.

We do not see her returning light
so much as taste it, a fine sliver in our mouths,
sweet and metallic, like the silver beads
which decorate anniversary cakes.
Then a thunderous sound, a rock
being pushed away from an underwater
cave, and her whole self rises,
belly up, gasping wind, snails
and hydra in her hair. Something
has changed about her; she's struggled,
she's given herself over. She's meaner,
clearer-edged, more beautiful and full.

We drift inside her light as if we are
her children, as if she will soon give birth
to the second half of our lives.
All around us the eggs are waiting, hunkered
against the cold in their glittered jackets.
The shadows have painted us as well—
orchid, azure, folding into black.

What My Son's Haircut Taught Me About Flying

The beautician's name is Robin Beebee. Wonder if her family was from down around our way? There was a Beebee farm where a sheep gave birth to a lamb with two heads. This was back during the Civil War before medical science could have kept a thing like that alive. They stuffed it looking in two directions. Not many in this town talk about the connection between that lamb with one body and two heads and the Civil War, when the country was nearly split in half. It is not a town for making sense of things like that—stuff it, put it in the museum, go on with your life. When Robin Beebee cut my son's hair and all of his curls went floating to the floor it surprised me that I thought of these things. Wishing he could have two heads, one for him and one for me. One with a real boy haircut, sideburns, straight line across the back, so he can feel good about himself, and one with the curls left alone, soft down his back like a little animal. We must fly in an airplane on Thursday, from up here in the cold to the warm south. The air is a place I do not want to be. I wish I had two bodies and could leave one behind here on the earth, sitting out in the cold cornfields watching the sky. But you can't have it two ways, that's kind of a town motto. Let the air do its business. Let Robin Beebee use her Beauty Academy schooling. Give your son to her. Her scissors are sharp as a taxidermist's and she has a smile on her face. "How's my little man today?" she asks. There was a time that lamb lay limp in someone's arms, breathing with two mouths.

Landscape

1
The dogwood, creamy, individuated,
is Father, right down to the transfusion-dot.
A pale-skinned man, quick to flower.
These hills are Mother, under her mossy
silk wedding gown. She throws the bouquet
and the whole western field blooms violet.
That setting sun, the cherry pie she dropped
on the floor the Thanksgiving after he died.
Fuck it, then she said, smiling with all her
teeth showing, and scooped it onto our plates.
Those three crosses up the hill behind
the Cut N Run Beauty Parlor, the middle
one festooned with roses, are flowers from
my Grandmother's only hat, pulled off to decorate
my wedding cake, a Lady Baltimore filled
with figs and candied orange peel.
Notice the fields of bloodflowers, the windshield
wipers beating against the rain. Grandfather's
story: Blooming red knicks on his customer's
faces after a quick shave, the beating of straight razor
against leather, steam rising off hot towels
as it does off that small, still lake over there,
unknowable fish beneath its surface like the barber's
unknowable customer, asleep, dreaming of water.

2
In the distance a glossy cow ascends the hill,
a soul wanting to find the highest places.
She struggles from the herd, then squirms
out of the landscape, a florid green dress
she leaves in a heap on the ground.

Now and then our faces appear
in the black reflecting pool of her warm side.
So full of old hope, our faces,
but the world forgets us, we forget
ourselves, and we're gone.
Soon the cow makes her way
into the rattling cedars
and she, too, vanishes,
and with her the narrative
whose pages once were edged in gold,
that darkening story, the world.

Mustard Seed

She was the bearer of the mustard seed necklace.
The seed hung suspended inside a glass marble,
a hardened, sulfuric tear dangling from a golden chain.
I wanted the seed, believed it was rightfully mine,
a legacy of my father's war years, a jewel
of adventure, not beauty. But she'd claimed it early,
and for good. There was no thievery stealthy enough
to outsmart the ballerina in her jewelry box, spinning
on its one white leg, net skirt twirling around its thighs,
striking up the tin orchestra that lived at the heart
of the box, alerting my sister every time.
The world colluded in keeping her treasures hers.

I did my best to stay out of her way, then learned
to take care of her to keep myself alive. Not take care
of her so much as serve her, spray the banana curls
with Aqua Net on prom night, pick lint off the shoes,
fill the blender with ice milk and chocolate sauce and puree
until it was just the way Derby Wilson, her boyfriend,
liked it. And when he dumped my sister I paid
the penance for her excess rage, let her pin my hands
to the floor and press her skinny ass into my belly.

I was such a girl when I was a child, letting it all
happen to me. In my twenties I would become
a real-live whore, the kind of whore fabricated
by the quick needles and tiny stitches of hate.
In the middle years I became a boy.
I carried a fishing pole, slit the fish down the belly
looking for egg sacs, and when I found them fried them
in butter and ate them as men will eat the liver
of the first deer shot in the season. One draws courage
from a liver, I suppose; what I sought from egg sacs

was the ability to learn my multiplication tables
and thereby multiply myself. I would become an army;
it would take an army to contend with her.

I searched for and cracked open geodes down by the pond,
still young enough to go to stones for lessons
in faith, still trying to convince myself that beauty
lies crystallized beneath the dull, bony skin of this life.
Back home, I ate like a boy, refused to wash like a boy,
was taciturn and solemn like a boy. I held an arrowhead
in my right hand in bed at night as a boy holds onto
his penis, to remind himself that he is his own weapon.
My bitter, golden seed waited inside me,
already coming to terms with the dark.

Running The Alphabet

There was not much of an inheritance.
A bed, but no headboard. A dog
the shape of a kidney bean who lived
for three days. It was the color
of a hush puppy shoe, a pair of which my father left
behind, the backs broken down from the nightly
pacing. Shoes and a picture of a rickshaw.
A picture of a rickshaw and a black stone
purported to be filled with sand. It was so hard,
so self-contained I was never able to break it open
to find out. A rumor of sand   that was his legacy.
I lay in bed when I was small, top of my head pressed
against the cool wall, looking for pinpoints of light
in the air raid curtains. Pinpoints of light, green-black curtains,
wallpaper covered in the huge blooms of the calla
lily. I had those things. A jointed snake carved
out of wood. A pile of cast-offs from my older sister,
clothes marked Petite whose seams burst
at the very thought of me.
I had stolen Maybelline, true blue, false violet.
And Yardley lip gloss, found in the parking lot
of the outdoor theater, someone else had used,
but only once. I touched the graceful furrows
of her fingerprint with my finger. At the empty
outdoor theater I counted the speaker-poles: 243.
Each row marked with a letter, not a number;
that was pleasing to me. I had the whole place
to myself during the day. The little train, quiet
on its rusted track. The swings shaped
like horses and jet fighters, I could pump and pump,
lining up the soles of my shoes
with the top edge of the empty screen.

Then the blackbirds came, scrawling in cursive,
opening their wings until each shiny feather
and its shadow cast itself against the screen.
Blackbirds, storm clouds, then, in my room,
spilled bottles of India Ink. I grew out
of my own clothes; I stripped naked;
my hair reached the floor. Under the sheets,
nightmares coming through in iambic pentameter.
What did I have? I had—you. All along. I could feel
your breath on the other side of the sheet. I could see you,
out of the corner of my eye, running the alphabet at the 31 Outdoor.
I imagined you blonde and poor, living in the underground house,
your bed invaded by the roots of trees. Your name
was the older root of my own: Diana.
You had a white headboard covered in gold flecks
patterned in the shape of the constellations.
I am now middle-aged; I have remained true to the black wings
of my eyeliner. Do you see me now, though we're older?
My face contoured by this very sheet of paper
like the flesh and bones of the child queen pushing
against her linen wrapping? I remember you,
an angel at the Pentecostal church, bangs too short,
speaking in tongues. I want to offer it back to you: my tongue.
I want to give you this, the second half of my life.
Will you look at me, although I am strange?
Do you see these winged monsters
shadowing the radiant screen?
They are blackbirds, they are the ghosts
of two little girls, they are my hands.

Sour Cherries

Before my first blood came I held my arms tight
to my sides, sucked in my stomach until I was
cutlass-shaped, my virgin cutting edge untested.
My blood was discovered by another girl, a girl
with so many sisters she was accustomed to bleeding
and what blood begets. The boys opened her
like a can of tuna fish; her laugh was tin-flavored
and she smelled like the sea. You've got blood
on your drawers, she said. Take care
of yourself. And she walked off displaying that space
between her thighs wide enough to hold a Jonathan
apple. You could tell from a girl's walk if she'd been
broken. She scared me, but my own blood scared me more,
the cocked-open safety pins, the pads with their translucent
tails like headless animals with two back ends. But bleeding
made me a woman, trusted with the stove, the red-hot
spirals of the burners, the sharpest knives which I used
to dice the onions while I cried a woman's tears. I held
raw flesh in my hands and learned to transform it, pulling
muscle from bone, trimming the fat, blood pooling and sizzling
in the bottom of the hot pan. I used the scythe in the field
between the rhubarb patch and the Church of God.
I learned to slice a wide arc through the air, clean-cutting
the milkweeds and thistles until what was left was a gold stubble,
like a blonde boy's face when he's forgotten to shave.
The moon carved a hole in the sky big enough
for its whole body to break through. I exhaled; my stomach
swelled through my clothes. Young trees bloomed
and fruited; crows pelted the Church of God with sour cherries.

Viceroy

My mother used to lock me out of the house
when she'd had enough of my shenanigans.
I'd have to pry the screen open
with a screwdriver to get my body back inside.
I'd stand out there strategizing, breathing the cool air.
I could see the fire of her cigarette intensify
when she took a drag, there inside her dark
bedroom, shade partly lifted, watching me.
The outside air was full of heavy yellow smoke
from the burn barrels, the paper mill, mushroom
factory, leaf burning. Hungry, I'd crave a potato
roasted in some roaring pile of leaves guarded by
a big sensible father. I leaned up against the oak tree
which had been split right in half by a lightning bolt,
open as a boy's unzipped fly.
It seemed like open always meant I was caught
in the cop's headlights in the vineyard
and somebody's pants were down.

Do you see, God, how I do not want to have to die
to get to come home? Being your child,
I want to be so alive that you gasp when I arrive.
You acknowledge the grape juice on my lips.
You light your Viceroy on the sparks in my hair.

Cat To Cat

When I put my arms around you
I felt something in you wither, step
back, fade a few shades lighter.
What's this, the lion is a pussy cat?
The white man gets whiter.
Under your glasses, cheek-tears.
What I had in mind was lion-to-tiger,
a little feline mixing of metaphors,
my striped dress clashing with your gold teeth.
I was ready to put my head in your jaws,
lose my brain to your freaky breath, climb
into the simmering kettle of your body.
Instead you knead my sweater with your dull claws,
wanting a wet nurse, a sugar tit, a nanny, a human
girl, Mary, opening the folds of her sky blue robe.
I want to be the kitty on the side, the one
drenched in sandalwood and velvet, the one
you think about later over your double-shot,
shaking your head, unbelievable chick,
a biter, and she wants to be bit back.

Hit

Batter my heart, three-personed
mud wrestler. If it be your will,
cover my body in celestial hickeys.
If it be your will, yank my chain.
I do not want your system of meaning,
the weight of your stack of dictionaries
balancing on my head. I do not want
to line up behind the ketchup-believers,
the mustard-followers. Let them argue
it out until their hot dogs are cold. I got
you under my skin like thorns under
fingernails. I want a direct God-hit,
no shrapnel. In other words, love,
I walk this dark minefield
searching for you.

Disguise

God could be
the slightly known—
an undertaker named Max.
The teenager who wanted
to kiss me. The woman
who sings Mustang Sally.
The short blonde who knocks
and knocks at three a.m.
looking for Frank and Dave,
asking can't I just come
inside and sleep? I could
have said yes. Made her
a bed on the couch. It
could have been one of
God's disguises, wearing
the blonde wig and the bright
green eyeshadow, hooded,
desperate eyes.
Oh how She knocked, loud,
with the flat of Her hand.
In the morning, that bright
lipstick print on the green
door. The pale pink glove.
High heel marks
in the snow.

Buzzards

I pretty much know what kind of buzzard
I am. Same as you, shiny black wings
and a red halo. Me and you, we know
what we like. Cook it up good and can
the recipe. A couple of instinctive cusses,
you and me. I can throw my wing
across your shoulder. I can cheat you
at poker. You and your hyena laugh,
your crazy pecker, beard stubble, hat,
cane, pocket watch missing the hour hand.
Oh we ride the rails. You and me, our cold
can of pork and beans. Our shared
can opener, so holy. Our gorgeous eyes.
Our genderless kisses. Our exquisite prayers.

Whole

I'm going. I'm going.
And I'm taking my precious corneas with me.
Unhand my kidneys, Sir.
My body, maybe, to the Institute of Bad Haircuts,
but never to science.
I have decided to arrive on your doorstep whole,
not waving my stumps to get your attention
or opening the severed breastbone to show you
my heartlessness. Bears don't give their hearts
away. Judge me as a bear. My liver is my own.
The dead should walk away stiffly, heads held high,
carrying all their toys in a potato sack
over their shoulders. Sack against bone.
You'll hear me coming.

Evaluations

Men by the quality of their shirts.
Women by the quality of their eyes.
Barbers by the quantity of bloody rags on their poles.
Beauticians by the quantity of hair on the floor.
Animals by tragedy.
Fruit by gravity.
Women by the grandiosity of their hairdos.
Men by the generosity of their bad news.
God by touch. Only touch will do.

II

Personality

Personality resides just beneath the forehead.
Round-breasted, like a small bird.
Green, but ripening, a lychee nut.
Colette brought a can of lychees to our dinner party;
she was sophisticated, perfumed, with a coral mouth.
We ate the lychees right out of the can.
I held mine in my mouth, whole,
afraid to bite down. Spit it into a napkin
on the sly, like a quail egg stained with ink.
Once the cleaning woman at work ran into the bathroom
and came out later holding her miscarried fetus
on a wad of toilet paper. She wandered around
the office like a ghost, showing it to everyone.
I was afraid if I split the lychee in half I'd find
a small girl inside, a naked child from out of the past
struggling to breathe on her own
because of something I had done, or failed to do.

The personality may be lifted from the brain easily,
like a quail egg from its nest in the weeds.
The lobotomized can attest to this. They are shown
a picture of a bird and they say taxi cab.
Their wedding rings, chop sticks, stones:
taxi cab, taxi cab, taxi cab.
When you know a person who has lost part
of the mind it's as if you have eaten a fruit
down to the center and found not a pit but a beautifully
engraved thimble. Inside the thimble, a fortune,
folded as if inside a Chinese cookie. You fear
it will mention the name of someone you've tried
to forget but no—taxi cab. Taxi cab.

I have known a few who managed to keep
a matchhead alive inside their cupped hand,
an egg, intact, fingers pinching down on the beak
to keep the brown nightingale from singing, from calling
attention to itself. They stuff their memories in their mouths,
chew and swallow the seeds and pulp rather than
letting them be seized. These are the ones who have burned
the cathedrals with their small handfuls of fire, who kiss
and pass a message, like a fruit stone,
from one mouth to the other.
These are the ones who reside inside my forehead, singing.
The ones I have banished when I wear
the robes of the coward, the jeweled
broken heart glistening over the left breast.

Hope

Hope? Haven't you outgrown that one by now? You think you're going to find a Baby Jesus in your Easter basket, in there with the black jelly beans? No, all you'll find in there is a few hundred bucks worth of dental work. But spring is coming, you say. You think God resurrects with the tulips. Instead of a pistil and stamen a little white man with two chicken pox on his hands? You're the type who clapped your hands raw bringing Tinkerbell back. Belief was like a bellows you could stick in her mouth, pump life into her neon body. Here's a bumper sticker for your collection: Crucifixion Kills. The rest is propaganda, it's what drives the American Machine, gets men like me to enlist and shoot old ladies in their sleep. I like your hair, though. I'd pour Drambuie in your belly button if I could afford a thimbleful. You've tried so hard, all losing battles. Guarding your daddy as if your will could keep the meat on his bones. Now his tie is alive with centipedes, millipedes in his eyelashes. You work your life away, all that curly red-brown hair I like to put my hands in. You think if you interview the babysitters enough all the children of the world will be safe? All safes have their safecrackers. Slick guys with intuition in their fingerprints. Technically speaking, I'm a killer, but I'm your loyal foot soldier, the one who'll bite your nails to the quick when you're nervous. I'm not what you'd call Jesus. Jesus wasn't Jesus. I'm the guy who walks in the door after hope has run off, tail between its legs. I'm the one wearing white clothes, vanilla yogurt in my bowl. Your jobs are minimal where I'm concerned. I do my own laundry, pull my own fruit off the trees. Peel my own grapes, whittle my own canoe. Low maintenance, undependable, I come with my own set of enigmatic tattoos. Don't count on me but don't count me out. See how I lick the tears off your face before they hit the pillow?

Scars are erogenous zones. Surrender to the bad man with the gold tooth and the wooden leg and the stars on the tips of his fingers. Your meaningful stories are music to my ears. Tell them till the cows come home, bumping against the house. The body is edible, drinkable, and you taste like mangoes and dark ale. When I'm done with you I'll have appreciated you. I know the way north. I go when I'm ready.

Morels

1
He's left, has been gone a while, now.
Trailing his moth-eaten buffalo skin,
his cigarette butts, the curling petals
of Love-Lies-Bleeding. Gone Fishing.
The Doctor is Out. Incognito.
He shaved his beard, shoeblacked his hair,
lampblacked his philosophical face. Low
to the ground, hunched, yellow reflective sunglasses.
Where headed? Well, West, for awhile, to the fishy shore
of Lake Michigan, a pithy one-ice cream-stand resort
where the local craft is carving tomahawks
out of cork. Yeah, cork. They float. And
so does he. He's done. Moved on.
With a funny salute as he drove away, the ravishing
shell-shocked Generalissimo of Losing Battles.

2
What do we do, girls, now that he's gone?
After we keen and rage, after his after
shave has worn off the pillow cases?
Here, where it is almost always winter?
We could cut an ice fishing hole, stare
hard into the green water, search
for the Devil. Once called, he'll never
stray. Certain to keep us warm, beyond
warm, at night. Or this: We'll drape
the blackbird robe over our shoulders and do
dishes. Clean up the joint.
After all that sobbing, through the steam
rising from the hot dishwater, we're sure to have
double-vision. We'll watch the sun rise

39

like an egg with two yolks. Twins.
Two cheese sandwiches for lunch. Two
mouths. Outside, two thin streams of melting
snow. Two pails to catch the drips from the two
broken-down roofs which half-way shelter us. We
two. Four breasts, twenty fingers, one-hundred
braids in our lavish hair. Ok, then, begone.
Begone. Is there an echo in here? Go—shack up
with the blonde angel who runs the caramel
corn machine. We will search the ground
near the fallen cherry tree. Morels, enough,
with their funk holes, their damp passageways.
Pull them like water-logged thumbs out of the dike
and the smell of wet earth will rise up to meet us.
No flowers this year? Then mushrooms.
Wreathes of them, mushroom nosegays
under our pillows. Sizzling, almost black
on our black plates. Cheers! Cheers.
To unblessed food. To the one
that got away. To outlasting God.

Kansas

If a lifetime is North America then I have reached Kansas.
From here I can see it all coming. Hail? Moving this way
from the next town, the girl has dropped all the white marbles
out of her apron. Twisters? I watch them from far off,
meandering old women bending at the waist,
berry picking. Their deep blue aprons are full
of everything that can be plucked and taken away.
Fierce gray hair flying, they can drive
a two-by-four like a golden needle through the pink silk
belly of a sow. I see Joe the Reaper, a sweet slack-jawed
boy who's too good at his work, never misses a stalk or a beat,
sweeps it all flat to the ground. Behind me, due east?
Love, its cracked voiceless bell, its proclamations and declarations,
its lobster traps, buttery pots, thwacking harpoons,
    its Shaker furniture,
quivering on bony legs like a newborn colt. Behind me, the restraint
of small black buckled shoes, behind me—that God. In front?
Solitude, the great desolation. Hawkish, I am
a stalked stalker. Old, with my knife, my red bowl, my funnel,
my great black apron. Alone, thirsting. In front of me is where
I will cut the arm from a cactus and finally taste the green juice
I've imagined my whole life, the wonderful thirst,
    the bitter quenching.
I walk, into the scribblings of sidewinders, the screeching of birds
with bloody beaks, the sun, her dress on fire, lowering herself
into the salty arms of her blue, undrinkable,
    moaning lover, screaming,
shaking the earth, breaking up the furniture. That God.

It Blows You Hollow

It takes your bones to bed,
tongues out the marrow.
Says it will meet you halfway,
a hotel deep in Oklahoma
where you'll get adjoining rooms
and have a couple of nervous
breakdowns. It's a no-show, waylaid.
It orders the venison sausage,
the lamb, the infant in puff
pastry, picks its pretty white
teeth with the pins from your little
sister's hair. Churns you till you
congeal, till the cream goes hard,
courts you till you're court-martialed,
hangs you till you've got a hard-on,
bangs your machine with its hips till you tilt,
your flippers frozen. Your heart's a tilt-a-whirl,
throwing off steam into the frigid night,
spinning heartsick, heartbreak.
It dances close with its hands
on your nipples, immaculately conceives you
and runs off with the kid in the night,
wears five watches on each arm, pillaged
from your ancestors, innocent and burned,
wrestles with your mother, gets your father
to confess his infidelities at Sunday dinner,
puts its fist in the cake, picks the buttercream
crucifixes off the hot cross buns,
teaches brother to piss his name into the snow,
shaves his head, needles him till he's tattooed.
It grows gorgeous on its deathbed,
rises gloriously to the occasion,

wills you its curls, its secret codes,
licks your fingerprints like a creamy cat,
dies with the grace of the curtain-pull at the golden opera,
clasps its hands, kisses Jesus on the lips, its body
lit from within like a fawnskin lampshade.
And all you want to do is revive it. You'll write
circles around it, half-assed parables halfway told,
with bandaged hands, with all the bones
in your face showing, by god,
you'll make a religion of it.

Stiffs

My dreams are full of working stiffs. Meaty,
small-minded pricks with complicated lives.
Gun owners, with a list of whom to shoot stashed
in the bread box. I've squirreled my list away for too long.
I've fought history. I've made like a salmon,
swimming uptown. In the place where I was born
they've covered the faces of the old buildings
with corrugated steel. Covering, uncovering, covering,
they can't decide which way to go. I'm from the south
of the north. My old boyfriend is still there, a tree trimmer.
He was struck by lightning last year, hit him in the belt
buckle. He dangled upside down in the tree for hours
until they found him and cut him down. Critical condition
for a night, then he swaggered out of the hospital
and headed straight for the Nugget, bragging that his dick
saved him from disaster one more time. Backwards cap,
he's still looking good. I could move back. There's a lavender
shack with an indigo gate stained with road salt, waiting for me.
My sister would uncap the Ragu, pop, like surfacing
out of general anesthesia after my abortion.
I could write ungrammatically, I could end up with a guy
who likes to do it sitting in a chair, twice a day.
The academics don't want me anyway; more important,
I don't want them. Maybe they've already wrecked
my mind for good. Even now I search for a metaphor
which will get me out of this free and clear.
Here we write treatises on irony, while down there
they work in the Iron Factory, on the line,
sweating for it. I can't go home. That place is too
complicated. The underworld there makes this place look
like a bowl of corn flakes on a sunny morning. Skull buried
under the dismantled boards of the old fruit stand, you know.
People nearly making good, then getting drunk to celebrate

and killing some kid in a head-on, rotting in jail
with their chins in the air, no remorse. The asses get
wider, the carnivals get wearier, the carnival workers lose
more fingers every year. They point at the constellations
with their stubs. I don't have the complexion anymore
to withstand those constellations, or the wind burn I get
standing high on Cemetery Hill. Not the complexion
for that place but this place makes my skin crawl.
If I end this with an image, I end it under duress.
The gun's to my head and I'm being ordered to bow out
gracefully. Even placing myself on the lap of some
lowdown archangel with burns on his belt buckle is a lie.
There's no way out. That's the only way out I know.

I Am Not Lost

I've lost but I am not lost. Asked what I will do now
I have no answer. No plan, but a waking dream:
A woman wears a certain raw shade of blue.
She gathers hen eggs in a basket. The landscape is flat
as a woman with very small breasts, so small they stay
out of her way. Mine have been narcissists, craving
center stage; I am tired of these heavy risings. The wind
is warm. The yellow sky is blowing up a storm. A fierce storm,
but an everyday kind of fierceness. Her hands are not tempted
to squeeze and break the shells of eggs as I once cracked
hollow chocolate ornaments in the chic department store
where I worked over the holidays. When no one was looking,
the fine chocolate shattered in my hand. I was eventually fired,
but not for that reason—for a kind of arrogance,
the much-despised arrogance of the working class. Again I say,
    I've lost. My job.
Technically, I gave it up, as a horse, pushed to the edge
of a cliff by those who make ropes whistle in the air,
gives up its life by leaping and falling. Having lost, but not
lost. The flat-chested woman gathers warm eggs.
She's slow and serene. No one knows what she does
all day or the source of that unperturbed smile. Her hand
eases under the breast of the sleeping hen. She will find
something there; it will fit in the palm of her hand.
The storm is blowing in. She can hear the wind whistling
through the cracks between the boards of the hen house.
She built it—not well, but well enough.
Her destiny tumbles across the flatlands towards her.
A very small thing moved by the wind.

For The Philosophy Professor Who Believes
Nothing Begins Just Outside Town

In our first brief encounter you tell me nothing
begins just outside the city limits
of Kalamazoo, to which you've recently moved.
"Nothing," you say, and I know nothing
more of you. I have decided to study this:
where each woman and man mandates
the beginning of nothing. "Nothing," you would say,
your tires squealing like the little dogs celebrities
have taken to carrying to awards ceremonies
in their pockets, navigating the curves
of Ravine Road, past overworked fields,
gold tatters of last summer's corn
sticking up through the snow. Nothing:
empty air hangs over the space inhabited
by the barn that burned last spring like a sheet
hangs over the furniture of the dead.
What nests once filled the knot holes of that barn,
jammed with hairless mice the size of the farmer's
cut-off fingertip? Pumpkinland. The hugely fat owner,
face grinding and trickling forth
its grainy handfuls of pride and shame;
his mother, who started the farm seventy years ago
with a single packet of seeds, is wrapped in a once-white shawl,
older in her way than all philosophies. She's the cashier,
who weighs the heavy gourds and calculates in her head,
sitting in her recliner which will not recline, the room
lit only by windowlight, smelling of urine, old apples,
the gutted seeds drying in a pan on the floor, to be planted
next spring on the high field behind the barn which overlooks
Twin Lakes. A man drowned there last year. He drove his Lexus
from the Mermaid Lounge, parked it along the side of Ravine
and walked into the Michigan night, crunching owl pellets
underfoot but unaware of owls, of the small bones and coats

of fur they do not digest. Owls watched him walk into the lake.
The heron was asleep in its wide, low nest like a basket
made for carrying dried corn. Suicide, drug-induced stupor,
no one knew. Some vast underestimation of depth,
of darkness. It's very dark out there—no street lights.
You can imagine the color of the flames when the barn
burned—amber, like what drips out of tapped sugar maples—
up against a night unused to such incandescence, therefore
cowering like someone let out of the root cellar after a long
imprisonment. What burned there? The vertical sheets
of particle board painted with animals, faces
cut out in an oval so a human face could slip inside;
the piano-playing skeleton; Snow White, her lavender
party dress, her blonde wig, overlaid upon a small
pumpkin painted with her eyes, her lips. The Hall
of Presidents, a portrait of every president sketched
in black magic marker, yearly, on a fresh pumpkin:
Rutherford B. Hayes, both Roosevelts, Truman, Jack,
each resembling the other except for some act of artistic
definition, a mustache or sideburns or heavy-rimmed
glasses, each golden head filled with empty space.
The styrofoam graveyard. The mocking witch.
Barn swallows, sparrows, bats, like flying matchheads,
struck. Nothing, its chest heaving, leans against a tree,
making the small sounds one hears when nothingness loses,
and therefore becomes larger, with nowhere to go except further
toward the city, crossing the limits, walking
toward your institutions,
the ones for higher learning, the ones for the insane—
nearing your house, sighing its vast sigh,
a breeze that carries the scent of overturned earth, the memory
of mint fields, the tiny black seeds of nothingness planted
in you, patiently waiting for spring, and summer,
and the whistling blades of harvest.

III

Drummond

I walk the grassed-over ferry dock.
The boats do not land here anymore.
No sailors come ashore asking for company.
A dead beaver, its tail the color of tar,
rocks with the water. There are deer droppings
like piles of black glass beads. Grazing
at the forest edge, a white cow
with black lines around her eyes.
Whose cow, and who will milk her?
She's eaten all the trillium off the forest bed;
her lips reach for the few dogwood petals.
Here is a small golden dog dragging
its leash along the waterline. I lock myself in
to a house that does not belong to me.
There are signs of a woman here—a drawer
which holds only a white negligee,
a pot of bright orange lip rouge,
a vase filled with the poisonous rattles of sumac.
Whoever she was she left in a hurry.
Her red soup in its white bowl is still warm.
Now I see a small girl sitting on the far end
of the old ferry dock, sucking a strand of her hair.
I've brought myself to an orphaned place.
No bridges, no ferries back to the mainland.
No compass needle in a dark pilot house
pointing in the direction of mercy.

The Plains

Early this morning I drove to Black Shoal Cove.
There, in the wet sand, the footprints of a bear,
and then the bear itself, face-on. I could see
its breath, like the fog stretched between
the spires of the bridge I crossed to get here.

In the store on the way to the shoal the woman
sold homemade lemon bars. Powdered sugar
dusted her fingertips when she handed me the change.
Her false teeth the color of the sky. I could tell
her loneliness knew no bounds. She offered
to accompany me to the Finnish Cemetery.
Historical, she said, but impossible to find.

I'll find it, I said, and did. A few unremarkable
stones, a fallen cross, some crushed flowers.
Then a snort and an emaciated deer walked out
of the woods, faced me and put its ears back.
Checking me, pulling up shoots, chewing, checking,
swallowing, which made a ripple move through
the whole throat like a falling row of dominos.
The deer struck me as arrogant until I noticed it
limping, one leg broken and poorly mended.

The coyotes will get it. The owner of the Bear
Track Inn tells me that later as he's pouring
my coffee. Tells me I'm lucky to have seen
a bear. There are people who've lived here
for twenty years who don't believe in bears.
He offers to escort me to the Plains. No
way your vehicle can handle those roads,
he says. Standing water. But worth
the excursion; college people come here

from all over to study that place, supposed
to be nowhere else like it on earth
except maybe Sweden. They think the Plains
are pretty much what the Earth was like
when it was first formed, he says, cold
and lonesome, and he opens the little package
of half and half for me, pours it in my cup
and stirs it with his open jackknife.
Oh, but I will get there on my own.
The stones are sharp, he says,
they'll pierce your tires. Raincheck, I say,

and find my way out there, up to my running boards
in standing water, my stomach in knots.
I pee on the cold plain, the golden
grass stretching around me like miles of human hair.
What had he said? Coyotes, bobcats, even wolves.
The sky, the orange-brown of the tannic acid which drips
from the roots of trees. Crows land on stones
which seem to have been arranged ritually, by a society
of grievers. I'm surrounded by marshland, chirring
and trickling, and then Huron and the Bay.
The shoals, he said, are black, undetectable
beneath the shallows, tearing holes in the boats of rescuers.

Ears

The wind's blowing as it has blown
for thousands of years, here in this small
place. Small to have held so many restless souls.
Layers of them under my feet, turning to dolomite.
There are places, when the sun is setting, the dogwoods
flush the color of hawkweed. Herds of deer run
out of the woods like salmon upriver, uproad.
A century ago a woman shot an arctic owl
between the eyes. It was chasing her daughter,
talons ready to carry her away. There are places
I can walk if I want to meet them:
Child running toward mother who holds the gun
high. Owl with three eyes. There was a girl
who journeyed here long ago and was advised
to wear a hat. She refused; she was twelve,
without parents, the cold wind turning the edges
of her ears the bright purple-red of the rising sun.
Ears, now underground, overhearing me tell
all I have overheard, as the wind rolls over my voice
like water over rocks, as lichen grows over my shoes.

Shutting The Door

On the mainland, forty-seven miles
north of the island, I find Penny's Café—
pizza with spinach, feta and banana peppers
and a tall latté; women in black clothes
with tinted lenses talking eye-to-eye about tragedies
in other countries, and on each table
a pepper grinder, a bottle of scotch
bonnet pepper sauce and a purple carnation.
I can almost believe the island has disappeared.
No more wary looks from the woman at the general store
who tells me to shut the door, who states the policy:
you open it you shut it.
No mass graves under the limestone quarry,
a people evanesced by smallpox.
No deer lying on the roadsides, flesh
eaten away by crows, brown bones exposed
like the ribs of wrecked ships. No more
loneliness crusted in the corners of the mouth
of a man whose face is caved-in on one side,
who writes country music, he tells me, blowing
smoke out of the side of his mouth,
music about heartbreak, mostly.
At Penny's the food stuns me with its beauty.
Green spinach a nest for petals of white cheese,
rounds of zucchini in the soup,
their edges scored like coins. If I play
my cards right I can stay here, or a place
just like it, for the rest of my days.

I can forget about my father singing strange
and ugly songs from the grave. Forget about
my mother, with her downturned mouth, cutting
her mother's pork roast into bite-sized pieces
with a dull knife, begging me to shut the door
I opened. Shut it against the cold.

Island Fever

I left for the day, feeling a bit of island fever.
Now the ferry-master tells me I cannot return.
Not this time, lady. Whitecaps in the harbor.

I remember the acidic green-gold cedar, low to the ground,
the humps of white limestone. Further out, on the eastern end,
wolves who cross over the ice from Canada, the deceptive

black shoals. I remember the deer, who asked little of me,
only that I let the crows pick their bones clean during the day,
let the hoarfrost form on their antlers at night.

From the island, I watched the freighters pass at dusk,
watched them with my whole body. A few men
and all that vibrating steel, the pulsing engine I could feel

in the soles of my shoes on shore. The freighter
rode low in the water, heavy with glossy black taconite,
like the pellets of wild animals shoveled into the hold.

From the island the world of men was quiet and distant
and strung with flickering white lights as if the cold prow
of space were hung with planets, a drifting solar system

I could watch through my telescope. In the harbor,
the angry red buoy dives deep and rolls high with the swells.
A skin of light breaks apart on the water, like the white bread

I would have crumbled and fed to the hungry
birds tonight, the gulls, the white-winged mergansers,
the loons, their eyes bloodshot from all that crying.

Quarry

I overhear it in the store and tell it
as if it were my story: an accident
last night at the dolomite quarry.
He was twenty-three, lived here
all his life. Just started his job
two weeks ago. The guys are so broken
up about it they closed down the quarry
for the day. Airlifted him to the Sault.
Crushed from the waist down. I repeat it
to whomever will listen. I like the feeling
of breaking bad news that is not my bad news.
Something about the story, telling it,
makes me feel like I really live here.
And yet, with each telling, I find I am
embellishing more, he's crushed
from the neck down, the guy who ran over
him was his best friend, they'd all told him
to never get out of the truck but he got out
of the truck. Let's not lay blame, I say.
Finally, it's me who was driving the truck.
Me, and I have banished myself from the island.
I've packed a few things and am leaving tomorrow
on the first ferry out. You mess up that big in a place
like this you might as well hang yourself.
In fact, I am planning to hang myself.
Who do you think that was, the man whose life I stole?
Jesus, I tell them. The Living Christ.
Yes, I tell them. You've met the cornerstone
of the whole bloody tale.

Deer On Drummond

run in trinities, three going together
like girlfriends watching each other's
back because it's a hard life up here
whip marks on their coats from nine
months in the thick of things
sometimes there's a crust of ice
over the snow so solid they can't break
through and snap their leg bones trying
you wouldn't call these girls gentle
with their long legs and swollen pudenda
window rolled down i say out loud
i'm not going to hurt you sister
like words matter
ears twitch and she stares my way
for awhile then squats to pee
a warm stream of it into the cattails
that mary mother of god look on her face:
i've lost so much but i must keep chewing

Sheath

Like a hand slipped from a glove I slip
out of my old life. A warm, fleece-lined glove.
Like a cicada from its ambergris shell. Shell so fragrant.
Like a sandhill crane from its nest of brown-spotted
eggs. Dry nest in the tundra grass. I live here now.
Not a soul here cares whether I live or die.
No one touches my face or reaches inside
the holes in my words. No one will emulate
my hair-do or care whether I walk out into the wilderness
on the northern end of the island and never return.
If someone came upon my body they'd move it with the end
of their boot. Coyotes got it, they'd say. That easily a woman
can shed her skin, like a birch tree, its great papery
sheath on which no story will ever be written.
Each naked tree winnowed down to its original loneliness.

Potatoes

The magic with which I credit myself,
the supernatural events I catalogue,
such small potatoes. Seeking wolves
and finding a pair, minor premonitions:
potatoes.
Fear is the only boundary.
The dead would come in droves, carried
in the talons of eagles.
The ones with smallpox scars on their faces
would climb out of the ground and drape
their blankets over my shoulders.
The wolf would crash through my windshield
with a radiant halo in its mouth. If not for fear.
The man at the bait and tackle shop
who opens the pinball game with a green key
and racks up nine free games for my pleasure
would unbutton and open his shirt to show me
his heart, ensnared in a wreath of thorns, crowned
in the petals of snow trillium, edged in flame.

Maker

It's up to me. I can drive out to the plains
past sundown and meet whomever I choose.
My father will wait for me on a large black stone
if I can bear to see him again. I can face
all the people my people betrayed, three to a stone.
I can meet my Maker if I wish, if I'm ready,
just lie down in the broomgrass and wait for the bobcats,
who purr before they strike. I can meet silence
more vast than God; it's what Jesus heard when he asked
why he'd been forsaken. Tonight, I'll do what he did.
Drive to the east of my greatest fear, into my deepest need.

Let's Name It Mary

Out of black rock grows the improbable smoke-colored grass.
Across it walks the split-hooved Mary. One of her legs
    is badly broken.
She limps, being the Mary that will never heal.
Her neck reaches down, her black lips pull what she finds there
into her mouth. She's the doomed chewer.
And then comes the little Mary who refused to wear a hat
when she made the crossing. Her hair thick and damp and gold
    as tundra grass,
blowing out from her face in glittering spires as she crossed
    the Georgian Bay.
And the Mary from the store, whose face is red from
    too much whiskey.
She's the one who came out here and nailed a little sign
    to a birch tree:
Mary, it said. And Smallpox Mary, wrapped in her
    tainted blanket, holding
a cold stone in her mouth to keep her tongue from burning.
Here rises the winged Mary, rust-colored, her voice like a rattle
stuck low in her long neck. Every animal here, a Mary.
Shall we name the island Mary? Here comes the old Mary,
walking with bleeding feet, searching for her lost lamb.

The Crossing

The cold crossing. Ferry-master
tips his hat, a cormorant on his shoulder.
I disembark upon a ragged shore.
Crisp gray moss under my feet;
I worry, as I walk, that I am crushing fine bones.
Swollen cattails showing their fur.
There is mystery here:
Who is stacking the stones on Maxton Plains?
Jesus comes here for his yearly tempting.
Two wolves use their noses to open a deer's ribcage.
The angels wear dresses made of flax grown on this place.
Grown, soaked, beaten, spun, dyed, weaved.
Another mystery: Who is the dressmaker?
Naked canes of the pussywillow the color of red licorice.
The cormorants again, a whole flock among the bleating lambs.
At night the animals trade bodies. The bear wobbling around
on the long legs of the deer. Rabbit squeezing into shrew.
Deer flying with the wings of the cormorant.
But they cannot trade the nature of their hungers.
Thus the wolf, dressed as a sheep, still drinks
from the neck of the deer. And I with my habit
of yearning. The little museum of our former lives
has collapsed under the weight of the snow.
All the artifacts, crushed to a fine powder.
Even the ferry ride seems so long ago.
Crossing St. Mary's River. Barely a mile.
Such a short distance, from life to afterlife.

Crossing Back

The harbor is smooth as bone.
The River Mary flows east, pushing
against the gray muscle of Huron
toward the island. She's always
at cross purposes with the grand
design. Gulls jackknife into
the water. Look at the buoy,
inert as a church spire. The ferry
lowers the plank; a new ferry-master,
much less skeletal than the old,
motions me aboard. Could it be
that something still waits for me,
open-armed, on that other shore?

Photo by Rebecca Klinepeter

Diane Seuss was raised in Niles, Michigan and has lived in New York and Cincinnati. She has published poetry in Alaska Quarterly Review, Poetry Northwest, Tamaqua, Northwest Review, Primavera, Exquisite Corpse, Passages North and Third Coast. Her work was also included in A Loving Testimony: Remembering Loved Ones Lost to AIDS. In 1995 she received a fellowship for a residency with the Atlantic Center for the Arts in Florida. She was the first recipient of the Jewel Heart Poetry Prize, and read from her poems at the University of Michigan with Allen Ginsberg and Patti Smith. Seuss teaches in the Creative Writing Program at Kalamazoo College in Michigan.